MESOAMERICAN MYTHOLOGY

GRAHAM FAIELLA

The Rosen Publishing Group, Inc., New York

Published in 2006 by The Rosen Publishing Group, Inc.
29 East 21st Street, New York, NY 10010

First Edition

Library of Congress Cataloging-in-Publication Data

Faiella, Graham.
Mesoamerican mythology / Graham Faiella.
    p. cm.—(Mythology around the world)
Includes bibliographical references.
ISBN 1-4042-0772-4 (lib. bdg.)
1. Aztec mythology. 2. Maya mythology. 3. Indian mythology—Mexico.
4. Indian mythology—Central America.
I. Title. II. Series.
F1219.76.R45F35 2005
398.2'089'97—dc22

                                                    2005014592

Manufactured in the United States of America

On the cover: An Aztec rendition of the god Quetzalcoatl.

CONTENTS

INTRODUCTION

The term "Mesoamerica" refers to a part of the region that today we call Central America, which was populated by various ancient civilizations. The region stretched from the highlands of central and southern Mexico to the lowlands of the Yucatán Peninsula, the highlands of Guatemala to Belize on the Caribbean coast, and down to parts of Honduras, El Salvador, and Costa Rica. Civilizations evolved in Mesoamerica for 2,750 years starting from about 1500 BC. The most influential were the Maya and the Aztecs.

The mythology of the Aztecs and the Maya is complex and colorful. Mayan mythology dates from thousands of years ago. The Aztecs had their own mythology but also borrowed myths from different Mesoamerican cultures

This stone carving and pyramid are from El Castillo (The Castle) in Chichén Itzá, Mexico.

before them. Our knowledge of Mayan and Aztec mythology comes from records made by the Spanish, original documents, sculptures and paintings, and the ruins of their cities and temples.

A myth is a story that is created by people to help them understand whatever they cannot easily explain otherwise, such as where they came from, how the world came to be, and natural phenomena like thunder and lightning, and the changing of seasons. For these people, myths serve as explanations for the world around them. Myths are different from tales because people believe myths are true. In this way, myths are closely related to religion; accepting them as truth requires faith. The myths, then, represent people's beliefs about themselves and their surroundings. They also offer insight into the culture and traditions of the people who created them.

Ancient Mesoamericans believed they were at the center of the universe. Everything in their universe revolved around them. Mythology was a way of putting the universe, and ancient peoples' relationship with it, into some kind of order. Mythology gave structure and meaning to their lives. Mesoamerican mythology described how the gods created human beings; how earlier worlds were created and destroyed; how food for the human race was discovered; what happened in the underworld of death; what made the sun, the moon, and the stars, and how they moved; how time itself moved in great cycles; and who the gods were, what they were like, and how they appeared to people in their daily lives.

1 MESOAMERICAN CULTURES AND CIVILIZATIONS

Throughout the history of Mesoamerica, different tribes, cultures, and civilizations emerged, rose to power, and declined. There was a lot of contact among different groups, including through warfare, political alliances, and trade. People migrated around the region. Cultural features came to be adopted and shared among different societies. The Aztecs were the most unified and powerful empire at the end of Mesoamerican history. The origins of the Maya date from before 1000 BC. The peak of their civilization was between AD 250 and AD 900. Although they declined after that, Mayan culture and mythology have survived to this day.

Olmecs

The Olmecs were the earliest Mesoamerican civilization. They lived in tropical lowlands on

Shown here is an Olmec statue in San Lorenzo, near Veracruz, Mexico.

Monte Albán, the excavation site of which is shown here, was one of the great cities of the Zapotec and Mixtec peoples. The city sat on the spot that is today's Oaxaca, Mexico. This site contains the ruins of great plazas, pyramids, underground passageways, and approximately 170 tombs.

the Gulf of Mexico coast. By around 1200 BC, the Olmecs were building ceremonial temples and huge stone sculptures to worship their gods and rulers. The Olmec civilization was the origin of many deities later incorporated by other Mesoamerican cultures.

Zapotecs

Olmec culture ended around 400 BC. The Zapotecs (meaning the "Cloud People"), from the highlands of Oaxaca (wah-HAH-ka) in

The Pyramid of the Sun, shown here, dominates the ruins of Teotihuacán. The pyramid rises 216 feet (66 meters) above ground level, and is approximately 720 by 760 feet (220 by 230 m) across at its base. Beneath the pyramid is a system of caves and tunnels, which were eventually discovered to have run throughout this ancient city.

southern Mexico, flourished from the time the Olmecs declined. They had a calendar and a writing system. The Zapotec capital of Monte Albán, built around 500 BC, was abandoned suddenly around AD 800.

Teotihuacán

Teotihuacán (te-oh-tee-wah-KAHN), meaning "city of the gods" or "place where the gods were created," was a powerful Meso-american city-state. This huge city of eight square miles (twenty-one square kilometers) had a population of up to 200,000 people. It flourished from the first century BC to the eighth century AD. Its influence was felt as far south as the Yucatán Peninsula by the Maya. In Aztec mythology, Teotihuacán was believed to be the birthplace of the gods and the origin of humankind. Teotihuacán gods included Quetzalcoatl (ket-zahl-co-WATL), the plumed serpent god who appeared throughout Mesoamerican mythologies.

Toltecs

Around the time of the decline of the Zapotecs and the Teotihuacán city-state (AD 850–900), the Toltecs moved from northwest Mesoamerica to the central Mexican highlands. There, in AD 968, according to Aztec legend, they established a capital city called Tollán (or Tula, as it is called today). Tollán later represented, for both the Aztecs and the Maya, a place of mythic beauty and glory. The Aztecs admired the Toltecs as a role model for the Aztecs' own ambitions to create a powerful Mesoamerican empire.

Maya

Around 2500 BC, a group of people with a common language migrated south from North America. They eventually settled in the Mesoamerican lowlands of what we know today as Guatemala. From there they split into a number of tribes around the Yucatán Peninsula, southern Mexico (the states of Chiapas and Tabasco today), Belize, Honduras, and El Salvador. These were the Maya, a diverse

Point
Ante
of th
Room
1, B

The Mayan civilization had been one of the greatest in the history of the Western Hemisphere. This sixteenth-century painting depicts Mayan priests and nobles judging prisoners of war. The Mayan reach and influence were vast. At the height of their civilization, the Mayan people occupied territory from southern Mexico to northern Belize.

group of people who created a rich civilization and mythology, which have survived to this day. Their territory extended more than 50,000 square miles (129,000 sq km). They flourished particularly from 100 BC through AD 900. What we know of Mayan mythology comes mainly from the so-called classic Maya period (AD 300–900). The best-known Mayan mythology comes from the Quiché (kee-CHAY) Maya of Guatemala.

Mayan cities were built around a center of sacred ceremonial and administrative buildings and royal palaces. Ordinary people lived in huts surrounding the city. The four-sided center of Mayan cities had a spiritual meaning: according to Mayan mythology, the sky was held up above Earth at the four cardinal points of the compass (north, east, south, west). Pyramids with steps, or stepped levels, represented gateways to the supernatural worlds of the gods. Temples were built in line with the rising of the sun at midsummer. Stone altars representing Earth were placed in front of monumental stone pillars that connected the underworld with the heavens. Mayan cities were designed so the Maya could communicate with their gods through ceremony.

Around AD 800 the Mayan classic period began to decline. The reason for the collapse is still unknown. Rivalry between Mayan city-states and an increasing population without enough food, as well as civil war and weakening political unity are the most likely reasons. After the last classic Mayan ruler died around AD 910, the great Mesoamerican Mayan classic period ended.

Aztecs

The Aztecs were originally a group of seven tribes that migrated down from northwest Mexico into what we know today as the Valley of Mexico in central Mexico. The Valley of Mexico covered an area of 2,500 square miles (6,475 sq km). It was mountainous, volcanic, rugged, and sometimes dry. The Mexica (meh-SHE-ka) were the most important of the seven tribes that settled in the area after AD 1200,

This Nahuatl Mexican painting is of the Aztec ruler Axayacatl, who reigned in the fifteenth century. Axayacatl, shown seated on his throne in this fifteenth-century painting, was the Mexican god of spring as well as of new vegetation.

and the country of Mexico was named after them. The name these tribes came to be known as, Aztecs, was introduced after the Spanish conquered the tribes in 1521. Aztec means "people of Aztlán" (ahs-TLAHN), the mythical place from where they came. It included the Mexica and all the tribes of central Mexico that spoke the language Nahuatl (na-WATL).

Around AD 1325, the Mexica founded Tenochtitlán (ten-och-teet-LAN). It became the largest city in Mesoamerica, with a population of about 250,000. (Mexico City was later built on top of the ruins of the city.) At the center of Tenochtitlán was a huge complex of temples, palaces, and stepped pyramids. The main building was the Templo Mayor, a twin structure dedicated to the Aztec chief god, Huitzilopochtli (weet-zee-lo-POCH-tlee), and to Tlaloc (tlah-LOK), the Toltec god of rain. The Aztecs were fierce warriors. They made regular human sacrifices to the gods. The Aztecs, like other Mesoamericans, believed that death by sacrifice, to nurture the

Montezuma II, also known as Moctezuma II, shown here, was the ninth Aztec emperor of Mexico. Montezuma came to power after succeeding his uncle Ahuizotl in 1502. Montezuma's leadership was greatly influenced and affected by his belief in Huitzilopochtli, the Aztec sun and war god.

gods, was a great honor. Warfare, for the Aztecs, was the main way to capture victims for sacrifice.

In 1519, a band of 350 Spanish soldiers, led by Hernán Cortés (ehr-NAHN cor-TEZ), landed on the coast of Mexico. The Aztec ruler Montezuma II (mon-tuh -ZOO-ma) believed that Cortés was possibly the god Quetzalcoatl who, in Mesoamerican mythology, had promised to return after his death. For that reason the Aztecs, who were superior in numbers, did not attack Cortés's forces. Cortés went on to conquer the whole Aztec Empire, which ended ancient Mesoamerican civilization.

It took thousands of years for the cultures, civilizations, and mythologies of Mesoamerica to evolve. It took the Spanish conquerors fewer than 100 years to destroy most of that civilization. However, some of the culture of the ancient Mesoamericans survives to this day among native people in parts of Central America. Among their most deeply rooted cultural features are mythical beliefs that connect them with their ancient Mesoamerican ancestors.

2 CONCEPTS OF MESOAMERICAN MYTHOLOGY

A number of mythic concepts were common to all Mesoamerican cultures. These included: multiple deities; belief in the spiritual worlds of a paradise and an underworld; time measured in calendar cycles according to observation of the celestial bodies (the sun, moon, the planets, and the stars); and belief in the dual nature of all things, meaning that everything in nature had two different, and usually opposite, aspects, or sides. Other concepts included self-sacrifice and human blood sacrifice to nurture the gods and preserve the continuity of life; the spiritual importance of maize, or corn, as a staple food; a ritual ball

Pictured here is a Zapotec sculpture of the god of maize.

court game; belief in a series of worlds created before the present world; and the function of myth to maintain social order.

The Mesoamerican Universe

Mesoamericans believed that everything in the sky (the sun, the moon, the planets, and the stars) revolved around Earth. Human

beings, they believed, occupied a central place in the universe, which spread out around, above, and below them. The four cardinal directions (north, south, east, and west) and the center point all had sacred meanings in Mesoamerican mythology. Earth was a place sandwiched between and connected to the sky and the underworld.

Mesoamericans took great care observing and recording the passage of the celestial bodies across the sky. Most of life, including creation and death,

Death is a major theme in Mesoamerican mythology, as it is throughout all mythologies around the world. This breastplate in the form of the Aztec god of death, Mictlantecuhtli, is evidence that the end of life, whether it occurred naturally or by sacrifice, was an ever-present concern in Mesoamerican life.

was represented in the mythology of the Mesoamerican sky. Earth, the sun, the moon, and the planet Venus were the most important celestial bodies in Mesoamerican mythology. The underworld was the sky's opposite, in direction and role, and connected to it by Earth. Deities inhabited the spiritual world of the sky and the underworld, but some were also present on Earth.

Deities

In the Mesoamerican universe, everything had a life force, an inner energy, a spiritual being. Human beings related to the spiritual universe by honoring their deities. Blood sacrifice was one of the most important ways that human beings honored Mesoamerican deities. The gods had used their own blood to create people, according to Mesoamerican myths. People had a sacred duty in return, they believed, to nurture the gods with their own ceremonies.

Cycles of Time

As Mesoamericans watched the skies above them, it was clear that life was a succession of cycles: of night and day; of the sun, the stars, and the moon; of seasons; and of births and deaths. Mesoamericans recorded cycles of time from their observations of all celestial bodies. They used different cycles to create different calendars. Mesoamerican astrologers calculated favorable and unfavorable times and events, according to the influences of the calendar gods.

Mesoamericans used two main calendars: a ceremonial calendar of 260 days, and a solar calendar, like the ones commonly used today, of 365 days. The 260-day calendar was called the *tzolkin* (tsol-KIN) by the Maya and the *tonalpohualli* (toe-nahl-poe-WALL-ee) by the Aztecs. It was divided into twenty periods of thirteen days each. In the Aztec tonalpohualli, each thirteen-day period (called a *trecena* [tray-SAY-nah]) was named after the trecena's first day. Each trecena name had either a good or bad meaning. Astrologers used the 260-day calendar like an almanac to forecast days or periods of good or bad luck.

The 365-day solar calendar year was called the *haab* by the Maya and *xiuhmolpilli* (she-ooh-mol-PEE-lee) by the Aztecs. It was related more to the cycle of agricultural seasons and the dates of sacred ceremonies than to the 260-day ceremonial calendar. The solar calendar had eighteen "months"

Featured here is an Aztec solar calendar. The solar calendar was the calendar most similar to our own of 365 days. The Aztec solar calendar was divided into eighteen months instead of our twelve months, and each month had twenty days instead of our average thirty days. The five days at the end of the year, which completed the solar cycle, were considered "unlucky" days.

of twenty days each, which totaled 360 days. The five days at the end of the calendar cycle that complete a solar year of 365 days were considered unlucky or dangerous.

Each of the twenty days of the "month" had a name, as did the days in the 260-day calendar. The Aztecs numbered the years from one to thirteen. Each year also had a name taken from four of their twenty day-names: House, Rabbit, Reed, and Flint. (Every 365 days, the year ended on one of these days.) It took fifty-two years for any particular year (say, 1-Rabbit) to repeat itself. It took 18,980 days (fifty-two years of 365 days each) for any point on the 260-day calendar to line up again with the same point on the 365-day calendar. This cycle of fifty-two years—the time it took for a point on each of the two calendars to revolve and coincide—is called a calendar round. The end of every fifty-two-year cycle was a sacred event for Mesoamericans. It represented the birth of a new sun, or a new world, which was a central feature of Mesoamerican mythology.

Duality

The Aztec word *nahual* (NAH-wahl) means alter-ego, or alternative form (or aspect), of a person or deity. The Mayan equivalent was *uay* (ooh-EYE). The words expressed the Mesoamerican concept of duality, meaning that everything was composed of two aspects, or forms. Each aspect was different from the other, but each depended on the other. Examples are night and day, light and dark, male and female, life and death, the sun and the moon, and fire and water. The gods usually had at least two different aspects. Duality

Maize, or corn, was one of the most important crops in Mesoamerican culture. This rendition of the goddess of maize, Chicomecóatl (which means "seven snakes"), was created by the Aztecs. She was one of the most important goddesses in Mexico. The number seven in her name is a symbol of luck and the power of regeneration.

was the Mesoamerican way of saying that there are two sides to everything in life that had to stay in balance in order to maintain harmony.

Corn

Corn, or maize, was the staple food of Mesoamericans. It was believed that the gods of the Maya used corn mixed with their own blood to make human beings. Mayan art sometimes pictured human heads in the form of corncobs to show the close relationship between people and the crop. Myths about the origin of corn are common to all Mesoamerican cultures.

3 MYTHOLOGICAL FEATURES OF THE MESOAMERICAN WORLD

We know about our world and the universe today through scientific explanation and religious belief. The ancient Mesoamericans understood their world through myths, which similarly explained the workings of the universe. The world through Mesoamerican eyes was a vision of mythic-religious belief. It was as real to ancient Mesoamericans as our scientific and religious views of the world are to us today.

Sky, Earth, and the Underworld

The Mesoamerican sky was a sacred place. It was inhabited by gods and the souls of infants and people who had died in a violent or heroic way,

Mictecacíhuatl, shown here, was the wife of the god of the dead, Mictlantecuhtli. Mictecacíhuatl was the goddess encountered by the deceased who didn't make it to paradise and journeyed for four years through the underworld of Mictlán. She resided in the last of the nine hells.

such as a warrior in battle, a woman in childbirth, or someone killed as human sacrifice.

Mesoamericans believed that the sky was either a simple colored band; the roof of a supreme Mayan god, Itzamná (eet-zahm-NAH), meaning "iguana house," in the shape of an iguana and covered with symbols of celestial bodies; or a dome that enclosed the universe. The sky was a watery place. Celestial objects drifted across it at different levels, like fish swimming in currents.

The Mesoamericans saw the sun and the moon as symbolic twins. The planet Venus is, after the moon, the brightest object in the night sky. Venus appears either as the morning star, just before dawn, or the evening star, just after sunset, and sometimes it does not appear at all. Mesoamericans believed Venus followed the sun into the underworld, as an evening star. As a morning star, it led the sun out of the underworld. Mesoamerican astronomers believed that Venus was a symbol of danger or conflict.

Sometimes the sky was described by Mesoamericans as having thirteen levels. The Aztecs called the highest level Omeyocán (oh-may-oh-KAHN). It was occupied by a supreme god, Ometeotl (oh-may-tay-OTL), who was both male and female in one being. Both the Maya and the Aztecs believed that four paths radiated from the center of the sky, to the east, west, north, and south. Each direction was associated with a particular color, god, year-name, birds or animals, and omens. The Mesoamerican sky was held up above Earth at its four corners by sacred "sky bearers," whom the Maya called the Bacabs (bah-COBS), the four sons of Itzamná.

Mesoamericans usually thought of Earth as divided into four parts, which were aligned with the four cardinal directions. Four trees on Earth held up the sky at the four cardinal direction points. A fifth so-called world tree grew at the center of the world. Its branches spread up into the sky. Its roots reached into the underworld, and its trunk provided the earthly link between the sky and the underworld.

Mesoamericans believed Earth rested on the back of a great lizard, either an iguana or a crocodile. The mountains and other topography of Earth's landscape were the scales and skin of the creature. Plants, animals, and people lived on its back. The Aztecs also believed Earth was a ferocious monster, which they called Tlaltecuhtli (tlahl-teck-OOT-lee), meaning "Earth lord."

In Mayan mythology, the creation of the world was equal to the creation of a cornfield. The creation of a cornfield symbolized the origin of humankind in many ways and, because of this, Earth was thought of as a four-sided cornfield.

The Mesoamerican underworld was a frightening place of the dead. Its Mayan name, Xibalba (she-BALL-bah), meant "place of fright." The Aztecs called it Mictlán (meek-TLAN). The Maya believed that caves were entrances to Xibalba. There was no Mesoamerican religious equivalent to the Christian concept of sinners going to hell. With the exception of those who died violently, everyone in Mesoamerican cultures went to the underworld after death. Mesoamerican mythology suggests that the underworld had different layers or compartments. Mayan pyramids were constructed on a design of nine tiers, which may have reflected the Mayan concept of a nine-level underworld leading to the sky at the top of it.

Death

Mesoamericans believed that the great god Quetzalcoatl created humanity from the bones of earlier people that he recovered from the underworld. Death, in the Mesoamerican view, was, therefore, the source of life. It was a natural balance to life. Everything that lived grew from everything that had died.

In the Mesoamerican mind, death was the continuation of the life-death cycle. Aztecs saw the journey the dead took as a series of obstacles. The last obstacle was a river that could only be crossed with the help of a dog.

Tlaloc, pictured here, is the Toltec god of rain. His name in Nahuatl means "he who makes things sprout." He is often depicted with large round eyes and long fangs, features quite similar to the Mayan rain god Chac, who was of the same time period.

In line with many mythologies and religions throughout history around the world, Mesoamerican mythology enforced the concept of the duality of the afterlife, that of paradise and hell. Shown here is a depiction of Tlalocán, the blissful paradise of the god Tlaloc.

Dogs were, therefore, sometimes associated with death and the underworld.

The Aztecs believed that if Tlaloc, the god of rain and lightning, caused a person's death by lightning or drowning, the person went to a heavenly paradise called Tlalocán (tlah-low-KAHN). Both Aztec and Mayan children went to the thirteenth level, the highest, of heaven. Other people who went to heaven rather than the underworld were those who died heroically and/or violently, such as warriors killed in battle, women who died in childbirth, and victims killed as human sacrifice.

Day and Night

For Mesoamericans, the cycle of day and night was like a cycle of life and death. When the sun set in the west, Meso-americans believed that it began its night journey. During the night the sun passed through the dark underworld of the Earth monster. Souls of people and animals were thought to wander and roam during the night. It was a time of instability and danger. The dawn of every new day meant the rebirth of the sun as it journeyed up from the underworld. It was a sign that life and order were restored to the universe. According to Aztec mythology, there were nine lords, or gods, of the night. Each ruled approximately one hour of darkness. Thirteen lords of the day each represented one of the thirteen hours of daylight. The numbers nine and thirteen might also have referred to the nine layers of the Aztec underworld and the thirteen layers of the sky.

The Creation of All Things

One of the central concepts of Mesoamerican mythology is the mythical creation of all things. The Mayan and Aztec myths explain

Huitzilopochtli, shown here, was the chief god of the Mexica. Huitzilopochtli was the Aztec sun and war god. His name means "resuscitated warrior of the south." His other names were Xiuhpilli (turquoise prince) and Totec (our lord).

how the gods created everything in the universe, including non-material things such as time, movement, and worship.

The central Mayan myth of creation is also a story of earlier worlds. Both Aztec and Mayan creation mythologies lead up to the final creation, that of human beings.

One of the most basic human questions is, "How did I get to where I am?" Today we answer that question through history and genealogy. The Maya and the Aztecs answered it through mythology.

4 MESOAMERICAN DEITIES

The Mesoamerican concept of deities was complicated. The Aztec word *teotl* (tay-OHTL) means "a kind of divine spirit or energy." The Mayan word *ku* means the "quality of being sacred." The Mayan and Aztec words could also mean a specific god with a particular aspect or manifestation (form, personality, and character). Deities usually had at least two different aspects in Mesoamerican mythology, reflecting the Mesoamerican concept of duality. Some had many more. Some gods derived from the legends of important or prominent people who had lived in earlier times. The Aztecs had more than 1,600 deities, mostly adopted from enemies they conquered or

This fifteenth-century limestone bust is of Xochiquetzal, the Aztec goddess of beauty, sexual love, and household arts.

Quetzalcoatl, pictured here in this fifteenth- or sixteenth-century painting, was a major Aztec deity. His name derives from the words *quetzalli*, which means "tail feather of the quetzal bird," and *coatl*, which means "snake."

inherited from earlier cultures. The Maya had far fewer deities, only around 170 that are known.

Quetzalcoatl

Quetzalcoatl appears throughout Mesoamerican mythology. The Aztec deity of Quetzalcoatl was derived from a heroic Toltec ruler named Ce (SAY) Acatl (AH-kahtl) Topiltzin (toe-peelt-ZEEN) Quetzalcoatl. The Aztecs, who revered the Toltecs, transformed their hero-ruler into the mythical god Quetzalcoatl.

Among the Maya, Quetzalcoatl was called Kukulcán (koo-kool-KAHN). The Quiché Maya of Guatemala called him Gucumatz (goo-koo-MAHTZ). In Aztec mythology, Quetzalcoatl appeared as Ehecatl (EH-cahtl), the god of wind throughout Mesoamerica. In mythology, Quetzalcoatl was always associated with positive and beneficial deeds. He was responsible for bringing human beings into the world. He discovered and delivered to people their main food, corn.

After the Mexican Revolution (1910–1920), Quetzalcoatl was revived as a traditional mythic symbol of the Mexican nation. His name means "plumed [feathered] serpent," from the green-feathered

quetzal bird of southern Mexico and Guatemala, and *coatl*, the
Aztec Nahuatl word for "serpent."

Tezcatlipoca

Tezcatlipoca (tez-kat-lee-PO-ka) was another powerful and important
Aztec god. His name means "smoking mirror." The black obsidian
mirrors on his head and foot were symbols of magic and sorcery in
ancient Mesoamerica. The mirrors may have been "smoking" because
Tezcatlipoca had numerous different facets and was difficult to pin
down clearly. As a god of both destruction and creation, Tezcatlipoca
appeared in more aspects than any other Mesoamerican deity. He
was a god of war and of many other things. He appeared just about
everywhere—in the sky, in the underworld, and on Earth.

Huitzilopochtli

Huitzilopochtli (weet-zee-lo-POCH-tlee) was the supreme god of the
Aztecs. His name means "hummingbird on the left" or "hummingbird of the south." (The south was on the left-hand side, as the sun
moved from east to west.)

Huitzilopochtli was the Aztec god of war. He led the seven original Mexica-Aztec tribes out of their mythical birthplace of Aztlán
in the twelfth century AD to their final destination of Tenochtitlán,
founded in 1345, in central Mexico.

The Aztecs honored Huitzilopochtli with the blood of human sacrifice to repay him as their patron god. Captive enemies were taken to
the sacrificial stone at the Templo Mayor of Tenochtitlán. Priests cut
open the victims' chests with a knife made of obsidian, a shiny

Like many Mesoamerican gods, Tezcatlipoca, shown here, was a complex and multifaceted figure. He was part of the divine hierarchy composed of Huitzilopochtli, Tlaloc, and Quetzalcoatl. He was generally depicted with a black stripe across his face; missing one foot; and having a mirror on his chest, in which he saw everything.

volcanic glass. They then pulled out the hearts of the victims, skinned their corpses, and cut off their arms and legs. The flesh of the sacrificed victims was eaten by the nobility, who believed it was sacred.

Ometeotl

Ometeotl was the supreme god of the Aztecs, and was the source of energy that created all the other deities and all life. Ometeotl lived in Omeyocán (oh-may-oh-KAHN), which was outside of time and space, where opposites (dualities such as light and dark, sound and silence, order and disorder, male and female) were unified. His name means "two god." Ometeotl's male part was Ometecuhtli (oh-may-tay-COOT-lee). His female part was Omecíhuatl (oh-may-SEE-whatl).

Tlaloc

Tlaloc (TLA-lok) was one of the oldest Mesoamerican deities. Tlaloc was the god of agriculture, rain, snowstorms, and all forms of precipitation and weather-related phenomena, such as floods and drought. Tlaloc was equal in status to Huitzilopochtli. They each occupied a temple at the summit of the most sacred central pyramid of Tenochitlán, the Templo Mayor. People who died by lightning, drowning, and some contagious diseases were received by Tlaloc in a heavenly paradise called Tlalocán (tlah-low-KAHN).

This terra-cotta vessel is in the form of the rain god Tlaloc. Tlaloc was extremely important, as his cult spread throughout Mexico in the four-teenth to sixteenth centuries. In addition to being loved, Tlaloc was also feared, as he was believed to have great control over the weather.

33

Mictlantecuhtli

Mictlantecuhtli (meek-tlan-tay-COOT-lee) was the Aztec lord god of death. He and his wife, Mictecacíhuatl (meek-tay-kah-SEE-whatl), were the lord and lady of death. Together they ruled Mictlán (meek-TLAN), which means "that which is below us," or the Aztec underworld.

Mayan Deities

When researchers first tried to identify Mayan deities in the nineteenth century, they were not sure of the names of each deity or what they represented. In 1904, Paul Schellhas, an expert in Mayan culture, classified the gods by letters, such as god A, god B, god C, and so on. This system of identifying Mayan gods is still in use.

More recent research on deities' identities has allowed us to assign some Mayan gods with names.

The Aztec god of the dead, Mictlantecuhtli, ruled Mictlán, the underworld, with his wife Mictecacíhuatl. According to myth, the dead who didn't make it to paradise made a four-year journey through the nine hells of Mictlán, after which they disappeared or found rest.

Hunab Ku

The Mayan supreme god of creation, similar to the Aztec god
Ometeotl, was Hunab Ku (hoo-NAHB KOO). His name means
"one" *(hun)*, "state of being" *(ab)*, and "god" *(ku)*. Like Ometeotl,
Hunab Ku was invisible and had no form. He was more of a divine
concept of creation than an actual god.

Itzamná

Itzamná, or god D, was thought to be the son of Hunab Ku. His
name means "iguana house." In Mayan mythology, the universe
was a structure, or *na*, meaning "house," that was in the form of
an iguana. The sky was the roof of the iguana house and Earth
was its floor. Itzamná created Earth and the sky as well as all
the other deities. The Maya believed that he invented writing
and taught it to people, who then made him the patron god of
knowledge. In his manifestation as the sun god, Kinich Ahau
(key-NEESH ah-HOW), Itzamná was the patron god of Mayan
rulers. Kinich Ahau, which means "the sun-face ruler," was the
spirit of the sun during the day. By night, traveling through the
underworld, he was a jaguar.

Kukulcán

Kukulcán was the god of wind and hurricanes and the Mayan
equivalent of Quetzalcoatl. The Quiché Maya called him
Gucumatz (goo-koo-MAHTZ).

According to the Maya, Kukulcán served many functions and was quite prominent in Mayan life. He was a god of the four elements. He was also the god of creation, resurrection, and reincarnation. The Kukulcán Pyramid, shown here, is in Chichén Itzá. Chichén Itzá is a small ancient Mayan ruin in the Yucatán.

Ah Puch

The opposite of Itzamná was the god of death, Ah Puch (AH POOSH), also called Hun Ahau (HOON ah-HOW), meaning "one ruler," and Yum Cimil (YOOM see-NEEL), meaning "lord of death." Ah Puch ruled the ninth level, the lowest, of the Mayan underworld Xibalba, called Mitnal (meet-NAHL). He was often shown accompanied by a dog or an owl, Mayan symbols of death.

5 GREAT MYTHS OF THE MAYA AND THE AZTECS

Mythology has a number of common features in Mesoamerican cultures. It includes the belief that earlier worlds were created and destroyed before the present world, that deities created the features of the present universe (sky, celestial objects, animals, and plants), and that gods later created human beings. Myths recorded the migratory journeys of tribes from a mythic origin to their present homeland. Migration myths recorded all the earlier rulers of the people, up to the present one.

The single most important source of Mayan mythology is the Popol Vuh (meaning "council book" in the Quiché language in which it was written). The unknown authors of this text, Quiché Maya noblemen, wrote it soon after the Spanish conquest, in the mid-sixteenth century. The authors said it was based on an ancient lost book. Aztec mythology comes mainly from

This fifteenth- or sixteenth-century Aztec pot is in the shape of the head of Tezcatlipoca.

Quetzalcoatl had many forms in Mesoamerican mythology. Ehecatl, the god of wind, was an Aztec reincarnation of Quetzalcoatl. True to the inter-connectedness of Mesoamerican mythologies, Quetzalcoatl appeared in many different forms throughout a variety of cultures, including those of the Aztecs, Toltecs, and Maya.

translations of the Popol Vuh by sixteenth-century Spanish mission-aries. They recorded the myths, religion, and culture of the Aztecs soon after the conquest.

The Aztec Myth of the Five Suns

The Aztecs believed that four "suns" (worlds) were created and destroyed before the fifth one in which they lived. The first sun lasted 676 years. It was named 4-Jaguar, or the sun of earth.

The people of the first sun were giants. It was created by the four sons of Ometeotl: Red Tezcatlipoca, Black Tezcatlipoca, Quetzalcoatl, and Huizilipochtli. Black Tezcatlipoca turned himself into the sun. He ruled the first world. When Quetzalcoatl struck him with a stick, Black Tezcatlipoca fell into the sea and later rose up from it as a mighty jaguar. He destroyed the first sun by eating it and all the people on it. (In another version of the myth, the people turn themselves into monkeys and hide in the trees to escape destruction.) Black Tezcatlipoca then rose into the sky. In the constellation we know as Ursa Major (or the Great Bear) he appeared as a jaguar.

Second Sun

The second sun was named 4-Wind, or the sun of wind. Quetzalcoatl ruled it as the god of wind, Ehecatl. A mighty wind destroyed the second

Ehecatl was the Aztec god of wind. Ehecatl's name literally means "wind." He is another form of the god Quetzalcoatl and brought life to everything. After he became involved with a woman named Mayahuel, he also gave love to mankind.

Chalchiuhtlicue's name literally means "jade skirt." Being the goddess of water, she was often represented as a river, from which grew a fruit-bearing tree. This tree symbolized the human heart.

sun after 364 years. One version of the myth says that the monkeys of the second sun turned themselves into wild turkeys, to escape destruction. Another version says that the people of the second sun were turned into monkeys.

"Those who lived under this second sun were carried away by the wind. It was under the sun 4-Wind that they all disappeared. They were carried away by the wind. They became monkeys. And this sun itself was also swept away by the wind." *(Quoted material from "La Leyenda de los Soles" [The Legend of the Suns], in* Aztec and Maya Myths *by Karl Taube.)*

Third Sun

The third sun, 4-Rainstorm, was ruled by Tlaloc, god of rain. It was the time that people discovered agriculture. A mighty rain of volcanic ash and fire destroyed the third sun after 312 years. People, in one version of the myth, were changed by the volcanic eruption into turkeys, dogs, and butterflies. In another version, the turkeys of the second sun changed themselves into noble rulers.

Fourth Sun

The fourth sun, 4-Water, was ruled over by Tlaloc's wife, Chalchiuhtlicue, goddess of water. A mighty flood destroyed the fourth sun after 676 years. The flood washed away mountains and brought the sky crashing down onto Earth. The inhabitants of the fourth sun escaped destruction by turning themselves into fish.

While the floods spread out for fifty-two years, the gods rearranged the universe into four parts. Different myths described how this was done. In one, the creator gods Tezcatlipoca and Quetzalcoatl raised the sky above Earth. They then transformed themselves into two mighty trees to support the sky above Earth. Another myth says that the four Bacabs were sent to support the sky above Earth. In another myth, Tezcatlipoca and Quetzalcoatl transform themselves into serpents who tear apart the great Earth monster, Tlaltecuhtli. Part of the monster's body becomes the sky. The other becomes Earth.

Fifth Sun

Before the creation of the fifth sun, people were created. These included Tata and Nene who, like Adam and Eve in the Bible, were the first couple. They escaped the flood of the fourth sun by hiding in the trunk of a tree. When they emerged, they made a fire to roast fish to eat. The fire smoked up the sky. This made Tezcatlipoca angry. He cut off the heads of Tata and Nene and sewed them onto their buttocks, turning them into dogs, the first ancestors of the fifth sun.

The Myth of the Origin of Corn

After the gods created people to live on the fifth sun, they needed to create food for people to eat. The myth of the origin of corn describes how the gods created that food. The myth has many versions, but the basic features are similar.

One day, Quetzalcoatl saw a red ant carrying a grain of corn. He asked the ant where he got the corn. The ant, who did not really want to tell him, finally agreed to take Quetzalcoatl to the source.

They went to Mount Tonacatepetl (toe-nah-cah-TEH-petl; or the "mountain of sustenance"). Quetzalcoatl turned himself into a black ant and got corn out of the mountain. He took it to the home of the gods, Tamoanchán (tah-mo-ahn-CHAN). There they chewed the corn into a mash and placed it on the lips of people to nourish them.

The Creation of the Fifth Sun Myth

The gods had made everything ready for the creation of the final world: the fifth sun. The world was still dark. The gods met at Teotihuacán to decide how the dawning of the fifth sun would happen:

The gods met at Teotihuacán to decide which one would be the sun to bring the dawn of the new world. An arrogant god named Tecuciztecatl (tay-coo-seez-TAY-cahtl) volunteered. The other gods, however, chose an alternative volunteer, a more humble god named Nanahuatzin (nah-nah-what-ZEEN). The two volunteer gods prayed and fasted for four days. The other gods made a great fire in a pit. They called on Tecuciztecatl to hurl himself into the fire. But Tecuciztecatl hesitated. He was afraid. He refused to throw himself into the fire. The more humble Nanahuatzin threw himself in immediately, without hesitation. Only then did Tecuciztecatl follow Nanahuatzin into the fire. An eagle and a jaguar then jumped into the fire. For their bravery in jumping into the fire, the eagle and the jaguar became the two great military orders of the Aztec Empire.

Nanahuatzin was the first to throw himself into the fire, so he was the first to rise in the east as the sun. Tecuciztecatl followed Nanahuatzin soon after. The two suns shone with the same brightness. One of the gods threw a rabbit in the face of Tecuciztecatl, to dim his brightness. He became the moon, with the shape of a rabbit on his face to this day.

The gods decided they had to sacrifice themselves to get the sun and the moon to start moving across the sky. So Quetzalcoatl cut the heart out of each god. This sacrifice of the gods put in motion the sun and the moon. It started the creation of the fifth sun, which was called the sun of movement.

"In this way, they [sun and moon] exchanged with each other.
They separated from each other.
In this way, the sun emerges once,
He takes one whole day.
And the moon shoulders his work for one whole night."
(Quoted material from Mesoamerican Mythology *by Kay Read and Jason González.)*

This myth explains the reason the Aztecs believed they had to offer regular sacrifices of human beings to repay for the self-sacrifice of the gods, which kept the fifth sun moving and their world going. Eventually, however, even their world of the fifth sun would come to an end, just as the four suns had before it. The Aztecs believed that violent earthquakes would destroy the sun of movement, consuming them and all creation and time itself.

The Mayan Popol Vuh

Most of Mayan mythology comes from a single source, the Popol Vuh, the sacred book of the Quiché Maya from the highlands of present-day Guatemala. It was written in the Quiché Mayan

Human sacrifice, particularly offering a person's heart to the sun god, was common in ancient Mesoamerican, and particularly Aztec, culture, as was bloodletting. These sacrifices were often based on the Aztec calendar.

language by unknown Quiché Maya noblemen in the mid-1550s. Around 1702 a Spanish friar found the book. He copied it and translated it from Quiché Mayan to Spanish. Since then it has been translated into many languages.

The Popol Vuh is the Quiché Mayan version of the mythical creation of the world and human beings. The central episodes of the book concern the deeds of the Hero Twins. They conquer the forces of darkness and disorder so that people can live in harmony with their world. The final part of the book narrates the history of the legendary ancestors and ruling dynasties of the Quiché Maya up to the time it was written, under Spanish colonial rule.

The beginning of the Popol Vuh describes a world of darkness. The sky is empty. Earth is a calm and empty sea. According to the translation by Dennis Tedlock, "Only the sky alone is there; the face of the earth is not clear. Only the sea alone is pooled under all the sky; there is nothing whatever gathered there." The gods are alone within the sea and the sky. As soon as the gods talk about creating the world, it appears. "And then the earth arose because of them [the gods], it was simply their word that brought it forth."

The Creation of Human Beings

The gods created animals to populate the earth. But the animals "just squawked, they just chattered, they just howled." The gods, unhappy that the animals could not speak and praise their makers, condemned the animals to be food for higher beings. They then made human beings out of mud. But the mud-people just crumbled into dust. Next came humans carved out of wood. The wood-people were no good because "there was nothing in their hearts and nothing in their minds, no memory of their mason and builder [the gods]." So the gods destroyed the wood-people. (Quoted material from the Tedlock translation.)

At this point the authors of the Popol Vuh interrupt the mythic story of creation to narrate the deeds of the Hero Twins, Xbalanqué (shbah-lahn-KAY) and Hunahpu (hoon-ah-POOH). The Hero Twins go through many tests of bravery and cunning to defeat the forces of darkness on Earth and in the Mayan underworld, Xibalba. At their final victory over the lord gods of death of Xibalba, they rise into the sky as the sun and the moon. It is only then, when darkness has been defeated, that the first real human beings are made. The creator goddess Xmucané (shmoo-kahn-EH), grandmother of the Hero Twins, grinds up yellow and white corn and mixes it with water. Out of that she makes the first four people of the human race, the first ancestors of the Quiché Maya people.

The four first people, however, see too much too clearly. They know too much. They are too much like gods! The final action of the gods in the creation of people is to dim their sight. According to Dennis Tedlock's translation, "Such was the loss of the means of understanding, along with the means of knowing everything, by the four humans."

The four ancestors journey to a mountain called Hacauitz (hah-cow-EETZ) to await the dawning of the sun. Nearby are other ancestral Mayan tribes. "In unity they stopped there," according to Dennis Tedlock's translation, "and in unity they had their dawning there . . . There were countless peoples, but there was just one dawn for all tribes." The final episodes of the Popol Vuh tell the mythic history of the Quiché Maya dynasties up until the last generation when, the authors wrote, "everything has been completed here concerning Quiché."

6 REMAINS OF MESOAMERICAN MYTHOLOGY TODAY

In the sixteenth century, the Spanish forced Christianity on the Mesoamerican peoples they conquered. Central American people today, however, still hold on to beliefs from their ancient Mesoamerican past. Sacred rituals and cere- monies are still performed that echo the voices of their distant mythic ancestors. Mayan farmers still honor Chac, the ancient god of rain and fertil- ity, to ensure a good harvest. Caves in the Mayan heartland are still thought to be entrances to Xibalba, the Mayan underworld. Among many contemporary Central American cultures, dogs are believed to lead the dead to the underworld, as they did in the myths of their Mesoamerican ancestors.

This sculpture of the rain god Chac is from the Temple of the Warriors in Chichén Itzá, Mexico.

Contemporary religion in Central America is often a combination of Christian and ancient Mesoamerican beliefs that continues to evolve.

Creations and Destructions

Myths of multiple creations and destructions of earlier worlds or races of human beings are among the most common myths surviving from ancient Mesoamerica. In these myths, the earlier races of people are usually imperfect in that they are unable or unwilling to obey and respect the gods who made them. The most common methods of mythical destruction are great floods or other natural catastrophes, or attack by jaguars.

A contemporary myth from the Mixé (mee-SHAY) people of Oaxaca in southern Mexico is similar to the myth of Tata and Nene in the Aztec myth of the five suns. In the Mixé version, the supreme

Chac was an important figure in Mayan culture and was depicted in many forms. In the Yucatán region of Mexico, he was depicted, as shown here, with a protruding nose and large fangs and eyes, similar to Tlaloc. Chac also comprised four different god forms, known as Chacs. Each Chac represented one of the four points of the compass: north, south, east, and west.

god, the Old One, warns the one man in the world that the world is going to be destroyed by a great flood. He tells the man to hide in a tree to survive. A flood covers Earth and destroys the world.

When Earth dries out, a new race of people comes into being. The man in the tree comes out and catches fish, which he cooks over a fire. The Old One is angry; he had told the man that he must not make fire. To punish the man for his disobedience, the Old One turns the man into a monkey. He switches the man's face and buttocks around. He turns the man's children into buzzards. To be turned into common animals is the fate of human beings who show disrespect for the gods.

A Mexican folk dance recalls the Aztec myth of the five suns. Dancers first present the death of each of the four early suns. The suns come back to life with the power of the fifth sun, which danced in the middle of the circle. In the Aztec myth, the first four suns represent the basic natural elements: earth, air (wind), fire, and water. Each one cannot exist on its own, so each is destroyed. The fifth sun, the life-giving sun of movement, gives energy to all the elements to create life for them.

Corn Today in Central America

Corn is still a staple food of contemporary Central America. It continues to be a symbol of human life, as it was among the ancient Mesoamericans. The ancient myth of the search for corn to feed people is told in many versions among Mesoamerican cultures today. Many of the myths say that a fox or a coyote first found corn.

Corn, or maize, was one of the most important crops in Mesoamerican culture. Serving as a major source of sustenance, corn has also played an important role in Mesoamerican mythology, religion, and art, as depicted here in this 1924 mural entitled *Corn Festival* by the Mexican artist Diego Rivera.

The Mopán of eastern Guatemala still tell a story to this day about the discovery of corn by a fox. The fox saw ants taking corn from under a rock, but the fox could not move the rock to get the corn. Other animals wanted the corn, too. They persuaded the most powerful of the gods of thunder, Yaluk, to throw a lightning bolt to break the rock and spill out the corn. This, say the Mopán, was how corn was brought into the world.

The story recalls how Quetzalcoatl found corn from seeing ants carrying it out from a mountain. Among the highland Maya of

Guatemala today, the umbilical cord of a newborn child is held, dripping blood, over a corncob. The cob is saved as the child's own sacred symbol of food.

A contemporary myth from the Cakchiquel (cahk-chee-KELL) Indians of Guatemala recalls how Xmucané, grandmother of the Hero Twins in the Popol Vuh, made people out of cornmeal. The Cakchiquel say that a coyote was cleaning its cornfield when it was killed by a hawk. The hawk took some of the coyote's corn and ground it up. It kneaded the cornmeal into a dough mixed with the blood of a snake and a tapir (an animal like a wild pig) to make the first human beings. The Cakchiquel myth speaks of multiple creations of human beings. Like the ancient Mayan and Aztec accounts, it also says that the first people made a long journey from a mythic origin to get to their present homeland.

Naguales

In Mesoamerican times, people believed that all things were alive; each thing had a soul, which was part of it but, at the same time, this soul was a separate being. The belief in the spirit of a person, called a *nahual* (NAH-wahl) or *nagual* (nah-GWAHL), reflected the concept of duality among ancient Mesoamericans. A nahual could even change a person's shape into the shape of the nahual, which could be an animal or even a force of nature such as lightning.

The Chontal people of Oaxaca in southern Mexico still believe in the independent life of a person's soul, similar to the life of nahuals. They believe that the soul lives in a person's heart or breath, and that it has a human form. A contemporary myth from El Salvador tells the story of a woman who could change into a pig. At the full moon she kneels down on a rock. Turning three times to the right and three times to the left, she changes into a pig and frightens the other villagers. A villager hides the rock she kneels on. She cannot change back into a person and remains a pig for the rest of her life.

In Conclusion

What does ancient Mesoamerican mythology tell us about ancient Mesoamerican people? The most obvious thing it tells us is that people believed that the mythical world of spirits and deities was all around them. More than that, they believed that the spirit world was actually real, that it was incorporated with the material world of objects and things. Everything in the Mesoamerican world had a duality. Mythology was the mirror that reflected the duality of the world: the spiritual aspect and the material aspect.

Mesoamerican deities had form and character. Most of them had multiple forms and characters. They also were not perfect; they made mistakes. It took the gods several attempts, for example, to create human beings. The gods could be tricked, as they were by the Hero Twins in the Popol Vuh. They could be arrogant, evil, or cowardly, as well as humble, generous, and brave. They were, in fact, like the human beings they created, with many different aspects to their personalities. Human beings were created in the image of the gods. Myths connected human beings with the gods and with their spiritual sides. The human race depended on the gods for

The relics of Mesoamerican mythology have survived for millennia and will continue to last for thousands of years more. Each of the pantheon of characters in the cultures' mythologies, such as this Chacmool, or bearer of messages, has taught us a great deal about the Mesoamerican people as well as humanity itself.

their existence. The gods depended on human beings for their existence, since people created the mythology. Both were independent, but each depended on the other for their existence. Mythology was the glue that bound them together.

The world of the ancient Mesoamericans was regularly upset by natural disasters such as earthquakes, volcanic eruptions, and drought. The landscape of Mesoamerica was powerful over its people, with high mountains, thick jungles, deep caves, and the sea.

The tropical environment could unleash dramatically violent forces such as thunderstorms, lightning, and hurricanes. Nature, in all its variety and changing aspects, surrounded the ancient Mesoamericans. It constantly threatened them with chaos, disorder, and even destruction. Mesoamericans used the features of their natural world to create a mythological supernatural world that they could control, that was safe, and which they could relate to. Through mythology they created a mythical place in which they could live secure in the knowledge that they were the chosen people of their self-sacrificing gods.

 GLOSSARY

astrologer A person who predicts the future based on the position of celestial bodies such as the planets and the stars.

cardinal point One of the four points of a compass, such as north, south, east, and west.

celestial Of, or relating to, the heavens.

contemporary Of today, or in current times.

continuity The consistent reappearance of something, such as an idea, symbol, or icon in mythology.

deities Gods and goddesses.

genealogy The lines of descent of ancestors in a family.

manifestation An indication of a behavior that is made evident.

migrate To move, usually in a group, from one place to another.

narrate To tell a story verbally.

obsidian Black glass created from the lava of volcanic eruptions, often used in Mesoamerican cultures to make sacrificial knives.

omen A sign or indication of a future occurrence.

patron A guardian, protector, or supporter of people or places.

revere To hold in high esteem; to admire greatly.

sustenance Food or nourishment.

FOR MORE INFORMATION

Foundation for the Advancement of Mesoamerican Studies, Inc.
268 South Suncoast Boulevard
Crystal River, FL 34429-5498
Web site: http://www.famsi.org

Institute for Mesoamerican Studies
Arts and Sciences 233
The University of Albany
1400 Washington Avenue
Albany, NY 12222
(518) 442 4722
e-mail: ims@albany.edu
Web site: http://www.albany.edu/ims

Maya Society of Minnesota
Hamline University
P.O. Box 40313
St. Paul, MN 55104
Web site: http://www.hamline.edu/mayasociety

Mesoamerican Center
Department of Art & Art History
The University of Texas at Austin
1 University Station D1300

Austin, TX 78712

e-mail: mayameet@ccwf.cc.utexas.edu

Web site: http://www.utmaya.org

Web Sites

Due to the changing nature of Internet links, the Rosen Publishing Group, Inc., has developed an online list of Web sites related to the subject of this book. This site is updated regularly. Please use this link to access the list:

http://www.rosenlinks.com/maw/meso

FOR FURTHER READING

Beihorst, John. *The Hungry Woman: Myths and Legends of the Aztecs*. New York, NY: William Morrow, 1984.

Boone, Elizabeth Hill. *The Aztec World: Exploring the Ancient World*. Washington, DC: Smithsonian Institution Press, 1982.

Brundage, Burr Cartwright. *The Fifth Sun: Aztec Gods, Aztec Worlds*. Austin, TX: University of Texas Press, 1979.

Burenhult, Goran, ed. *Great Civilizations: Society and Culture in the Ancient World*. San Francisco, CA: Fog City Press, 2004.

Campbell, Joseph. *The Masks of God: Creative Mythology*. New York, NY: Arkana/Penguin Books, 1991.

Carter, Geraldine. *The Illustrated Guide to Latin American Mythology*. London, England: Studio Editions, 1995.

Durán, Fray Diego. *Book of the Gods and Rites of the Ancient Calendar*. Translated by Doris Heyden and Fernando Horcasitas. Norman, OK: University of Oklahoma Press, 1971.

Graulich, Michel. *Myths of Ancient Mexico*. Norman, OK: University of Oklahoma Press, 1997.

López-Austin, Alfredo, Bernard De Montellano, and Thelma De Montellano. *The Rabbit on the Face of the Moon: Mythology in the Mesoamerican Tradition*. Salt Lake City, UT: University of Utah Press, 1996.

Markman, Roberta, and Peter Markman. *The Flayed God: The Mesoamerican Mythological Tradition*. New York, NY: HarperCollins, 1994.

Miller, Mary Ellen, and Linda Schele. *The Blood of Kings*. New York, NY: George Braziller, 1985.

National Geographic. "Ancient Mesoamerica." Washington, DC: National Geographic Society, December 1997.

Phillips, Charles, and David Jones. *The Illustrated Encyclopedia of Aztec and Maya*. London, England: Lorenz Books, 2004.

Schuman, Michael A. *Mayan and Aztec Mythology*. Berkeley Heights, NJ: Enslow Publishers, 2001.

Sharer, Robert J. *The Ancient Maya*, 5th ed. Stanford, CA: Stanford University Press, 1994.

Townsend, Richard. *The Aztecs*. London, England: Thames and Hudson, 1992.

Willis, Roy, ed. "Mesoamerica." *World Mythology*. London, England: Simon and Schuster, 1993.

BIBLIOGRAPHY

Bierhorst, John. *The Mythology of Mexico and Central America.* New York, NY: Oxford University Press, 2002.

Bonnefoy, Yves. "Mesoamerican Religion." *Mythologies*, Vol. 2. Chicago, IL: University of Chicago Press, 1991.

González, Jason J., and Kay Almere Read. *Mesoamerican Mythology.* New York, NY: Oxford University Press, 2002.

Hernández, A. Arellano, M. Ayala Falcón, B. de la Fuente, Mercedes de la Garza, B. Olmedo Vera, and L. Staines Cicero. *The Mayas of the Classic Period.* Milan, Italy: Editoriale Jaca Book, 1999.

Jones, David M. *Mythology of the Aztecs and Maya.* London, England: Southwater/Anness Publishing Ltd., 2003.

Littleton, C. Scott, ed . "Mesoamerica's Gods of Sun and Sacrifice." *Mythology: The Illustrated Anthology of World Myth and Storytelling.* London, England: Duncan Baird Publishers, 2002.

Miller, Mary, and Karl Taube. *An Illustrated Dictionary of the Gods and Symbols of Ancient Mexico and the Maya.* London, England: Thames & Hudson, 2003

Nicholson, Irene. *Mexican and Central American Mythology.* London, England: Paul Hamlyn, 1967.

Taube, Karl. *Aztec and Maya Myths.* London, England: British Museum Press, 1993

Tedlock, Dennis, trans. *Popol Vuh: The Definitive Edition of the Mayan Book of the Dawn of Life and the Glories of Gods and Kings.* New York, NY: Simon & Schuster, 1996.

INDEX

About the Author

Graham Faiella has written nonfiction books about whales, fishing in Bermuda, the countries Spain and England, the Enlightenment philosopher John Locke, and *Moby Dick* and the nineteenth-century whaling industry. Originally from Bermuda, Mr. Faiella has lived in London, England, since graduating with an MA from Edinburgh University in Scotland in 1978. His interest in Mesoamerica derives from one of his graduate school degree fields, Hispanic studies.

Photo Credits

Cover, pp. 1, 28 © The Art Archive/National Archives Mexico/Mireille Vautier; pp. 4–5 © Angelo Cavalli/The Image Bank/Getty Images, Inc.; p. 6 © Nathaniel Tarn/Photo Researchers, Inc.; p. 7 © The Art Archive/Dagli Orti; p. 8 © Werner Forman/Art Resource, NY; p. 10 © Peabody Museum, Harvard University, Cambridge, MA/Bridgeman Art Library; pp. 12–13 © Getty Images, Inc.; pp. 14, 30 © Mary Evans Picture Library; pp. 15, 18, 22 © The Art Archive/National Anthropological Museum Mexico/Dagli Orti; pp. 16, 26, 37, 54 © The Bridgeman Art Library; p. 20 © The Art Archive/Xalapa Museum, Veracruz, Mexico; Dagli Orti; pp. 25, 33 © The Art Archive/Museo del Templo Mayor Mexico/Dagli Orti; p. 29 © The Art Archive/Joseph Martin; p. 32 © Werner Forman/Art Resource, NY.; p. 34 © HIP/Art Resource, NY; p. 36 © Erich Lessing/Art Resource, NY; p. 38 © The Art Archive/Bibliothèque de l'Assemblée Nationale, Paris/Mireille Vautier; p. 39 © Scala/Art Resource, NY; p. 40 © The Art Archive/Mexican National Library/Mireille Vautier; p. 45; The Art Archive/National Archives Mexico/Dagli Orti; p. 48 © The Art Archive/Museo Regional de Antropologia, Merida, Mexico/Dagli Orti; p. 49 © The Art Archive/Archaeological Museum Tikal Guatemala/Dagli Orti; p. 51 © Schalkwijk/Art Resource, NY.

Designer: Thomas Forget
Editor: Nicholas Croce
Photo Researcher: Hillary Arnold